PIANO • VOCAL • GUITAR

AMY GRANT
HEART IN MOTION

ISBN 0-7935-0834-7

Hal Leonard Publishing Corporation
7777 West Bluemound Road P.O. Box 13819 Milwaukee, WI 53213

BABY BABY

Words and Music by AMY GRANT
and KEITH THOMAS

GOOD FOR ME

Words and Music by TOM SNOW, JAY GRUSKA
AMY GRANT and WAYNE KIRKPATRICK

you pull out __ my danc - ing shoes. __ I think a you could be so good for __ me

'Cause you get brave __ when I __ get shy. __

Good for me ba - by 'Cause

Just an - oth - er rea - son why __ I think-a you could be so good for __ me.

So good.__

Could be so good for

me. You could be so good

Could be so good.

(Bkgd:) A - could be so good for me.

EVERY HEARTBEAT

Words and Music by AMY GRANT,
WAYNE KIRKPATRICK and CHARLIE PEACOCK

THAT'S WHAT LOVE IS FOR

Words and Music by MICHAEL OMARTIAN,
MARK MUELLER and AMY GRANT

24

That's what love ___ is for. ___ To help us through_ it.

That's what love ___ is for. ___ Noth-ing else can do ___ it.

{ Round off the edg - es, talk us down from the ledg - es, }
{ Melt our de - fens - es bring us back to our sens - es, } give us

strength to try _ once more. ___ Ba - by that's _ what love _ is for

Repeat and Fad

GALILEO

Words and Music by AMY GRANT, MIMI VERNER,
GARDNER COLE and MICHAEL OMARTIAN

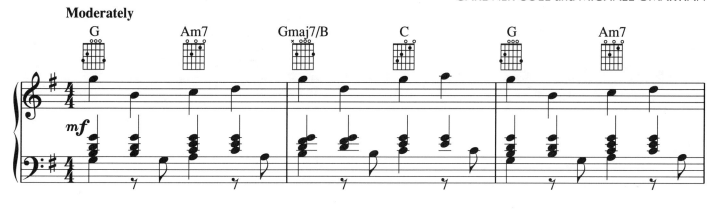

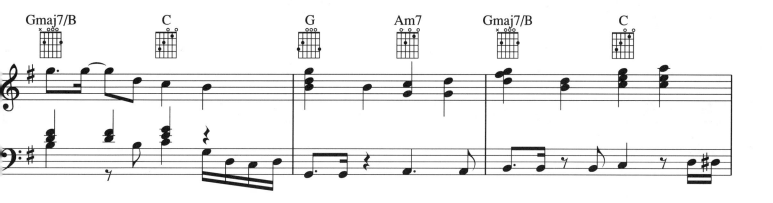

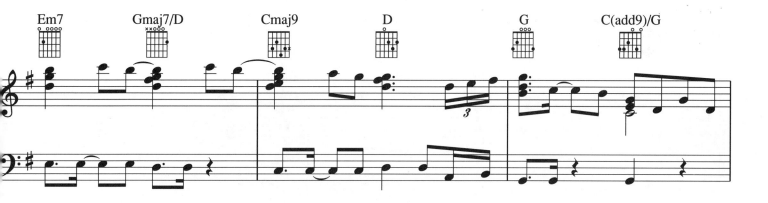

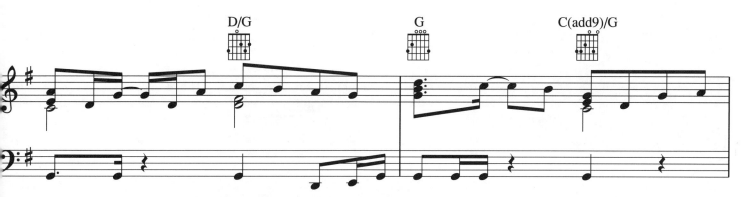

ASK ME

Words and Music by AMY GRANT
and TOM HEMBY

Moderately, with a steady beat

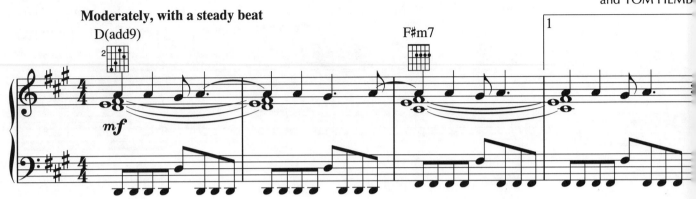

I see her as a lit-tle girl hid-ing in her room. She
look-ing in the mir-ror at a love-ly wom-an face. No mor-

take an-oth-er bath and she'd spray her mom-ma's per - fume___
fright-ened lit-tle girl like she's gone with-out a trace. ___

YOU'RE NOT ALONE

Words and Music by DENNIE MORGAN,
SIMON CLIMIE and ROB FISHER

Medium Tempo

I saw you walk-ing by ___ your-self, ___ you
The mo-ment that I looked at you ___ I

42

HATS

Words and Music by AMY GRANT
and CHRIS EATON

Moderately bright tempo

sun comes up, the break - fast show.
wa - ter is hot. The phone don't stop.

Well 1.,3. it don't stop. No it's
The 2. spir - it is will - ing but the

nev - er gon - na stop.
flesh is___ week.___

Why do I have to wear so man - y things on my head?

(Hats!) One ___ day I'm a moth - er One ___ day I'm a lov - er

What am I sup-posed to do? ___ (Hats!) Work - in' for a liv - in' all

47

be - cause I'm driv - en   to   be the ver - y   best _____   for you.

Gm7

Sax solo - ad lib.

C7   C7sus   1,3

C7sus   2

no chord   4

Solo ends

49

I WILL REMEMBER YOU

Words and Music by AMY GRANT,
GARY CHAPMAN and KEITH THOMAS

I will be walk-ing ___ one day

down a

Look in my eyes while you're ___ near.

Tell me wha

years come ___ and gone ___

and yet the

To Coda

56

HOW CAN WE SEE THAT FAR

Words and Music by AMY GRANT
and TOM HEMBY

HOPE SET HIGH

Words and Music b
AMY GRAN

I've got my hope set high. _____

1.,2. That's why I came to-night. _____   I need to
3. And like a star at night _____   Out of the
4. Be-yond the wrong and right _____   I need to

see the truth _____ I need to see the light. _____
deep-est dark _____ it shines the pur-est light. _____
see the truth _____ I need to